ON TOP OF SPAGHETTI

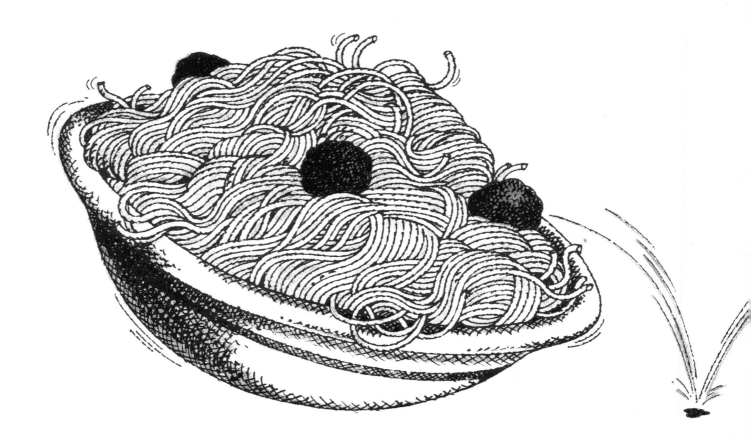

ON TOP OF SPAGHETTI

TOM GLAZER
ILLUSTRATED BY TOM GARCIA

DOUBLEDAY & COMPANY, INC.

Garden City, New York

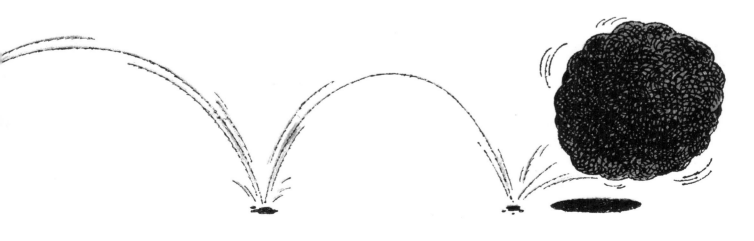

/

ON TOP OF SPAGHETTI
lyrics by Tom Glazer
music adapted by Tom Glazer
copyright © 1963 by Songs Music, Inc., Scarborough, N.Y. 10510
Reprinted by permission.

Library of Congress Cataloging in Publication Data

Glazer, Tom.
On top of spaghetti.

Summary: A parody, sung to the tune of "On Top of Old
Smokey," tracing the meanderings of a meatball that was
sneezed off a plate of spaghetti.
[1. Songs] I. Garcia, Tom. II. Title.
PZ8.3.G427On 1982   784.6'2406   AACR2

ISBN: 0-385-14250-1 Trade
ISBN: 0-385-14251-X Prebound
Library of Congress Catalog Card Number 81-43042

ON TOP OF SPAGHETTI

This Spaghetti is affectionately dedicated
to the Chinese who may have invented it,
to the Italians who made it famous, and
to the children who have fun with it.

On top of spa - ghet - ti,

All cov - ered with cheese,

I lost my poor meat - ball,

When some-bod-y sneezed.

It rolled off the   ta - ble,

And on - to the floor,

And then my poor meat - ball

Rolled out of the door.

It rolled in the gar - den,

And   un-der a   bush,

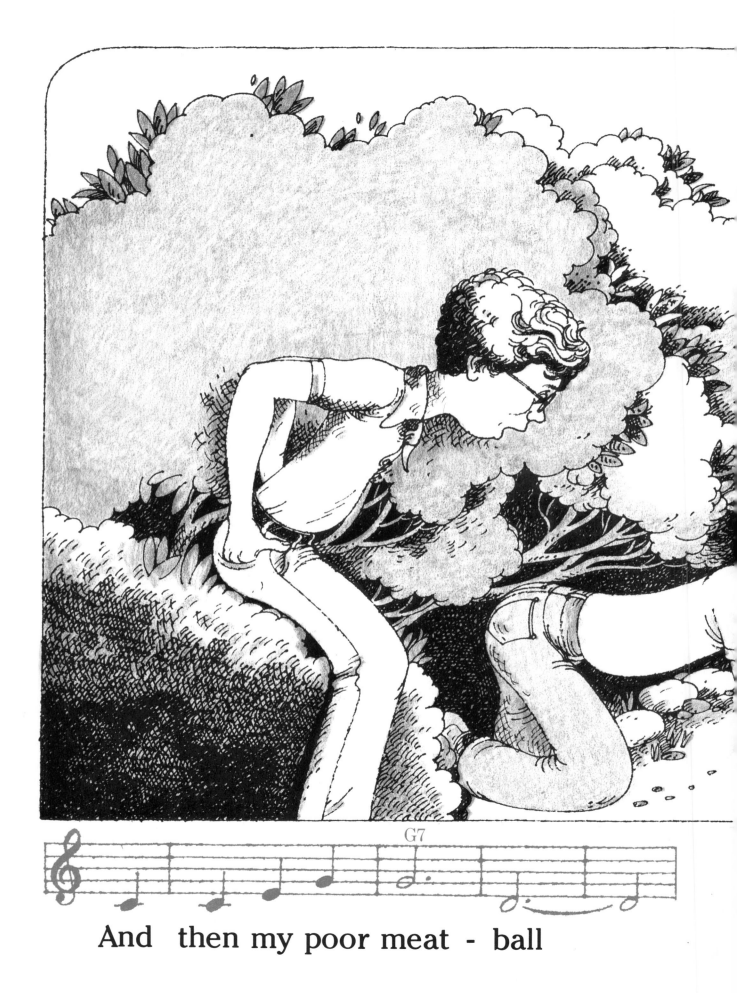

And then my poor meat - ball

Was   noth-ing but   mush.

The mush was as   tast - y,

As   tast - y could be,

And ear - ly next sum - mer,

It grew to a tree.

The tree was all cov - ered

With beau - ti - ful moss,

It grew great big meat - balls,

And   to - ma - to   sauce.

So if you eat spa - ghet - ti,

All   cov-ered with   cheese,

Hold   on   to your   meat - ball,

C   F   C

And   don't ev-er sneeze! (Ah-h-h-Choo!)

Tom Glazer is one of the country's foremost balladeers and folk singers. He began singing folk songs more than twenty years ago and has performed on radio, on television, and in concerts across the United States. He has made a number of well-known recordings for children, including one of ON TOP OF SPAGHETTI. He is also a successful songwriter and composer and the author of many books. These include *Do Your Ears Hang Low?, Eye Winker, Tom Tinker, Chin Chopper* and the *All About Your Name* series.

Tom Garcia has illustrated a variety of books for children. A graduate of the Arts Center College of Design in Pasadena, California, he also enjoys listening to bluegrass music, collecting antiques, and cooking. Mr. Garcia lives in Connecticut and shares his house with twelve cats and a dog.